MW00737685

A VICTORIAN CHRISTMAS

PHOTOGRAPHY AND DESIGN
BY KOREN TRYGG
TEXT BY LUCY POSHEK

ANTIOCH GOURMET
GIFT BOOKS

Published by Antioch Publishing Company
Yellow Springs, Ohio 45387

ISBN 0-89954-297-2

A VICTORIAN CHRISTMAS

Printed and bound in the U.S.A.

CONTENTS

VICTORIAN CHRISTMAS TRADITIONS

For all of our merriest and most enduring Christmas traditions we have the Victorians to thank, for it was during the nineteenth century that Christmas became the classic, festive holiday we cherish today.

Admittedly, many yuletide customs stem from rituals that originated long before Queen Victoria ascended the throne in the 1830's. The traditions of plum pudding, the wassail bowl, the yule log, mistletoe, and indoor greenery all date back to ancient times. Even the Christmas tree—a German tradition—began in the sixteenth century. But the Victorians revived all of these declining customs by emphasizing their romantic and religious significance. They also invented meaningful new rituals, such as the singing of Christmas carols, gift giving, and contributing charity to the less fortunate.

The Christmas spirit was further rekindled by famous Victorian writers such as Charles Dickens and Washington Irving. In the 1840's, Dickens rendered a vivid, sentimental account of the classic Christmas feast and holiday merrymaking in *A Christmas Carol* and *A Christmas Tree*. Irving's 1819 book, *Sketches by Geoffrey Crayon*, also romanticized the merry old English Christmas.

The magical myth of Santa Claus, also known as Old Father Christmas and Saint Nicholas, dates back to the fifteenth century. But our modern idea of a fat, jolly Santa, with eight reindeer to pull his sleigh, was invented by Clement Moore, who wrote "A Visit from St. Nicholas" in 1822.

Most of the well-known Christmas carols of today were written in the nineteenth century and were especially popular in Britain. "Jingle Bells," originally called "A One-Horse Open Sleigh," was composed by J.S. Pierpont in 1857. The lyrics to "Away in a Manger" were printed in 1885. "What Child Is This?" took its melody from an already existing one—"Greensleeves"—and the new words were written by a Victorian Scotsman.

In Victorian times, the yule season lasted for the twelve days following Christmas Eve to Twelfth Night— not the preceding month, as nowadays. The yule log, a large log put on the hearth beginning Christmas Eve, was burned throughout this period. Also during the yule season, the wassail (a drink made from mulled ale, wine or cider, eggs, roasted apples, and spices) was offered to passing carolers.

In America it took longer for Christmas to shake off its Puritan austerity and evolve into a time when traditional greenery, feasting, gifts and, most of all, the sharing of good cheer with family and friends were celebrated. As more Anglican and European immigrants settled in America, Christmas grew quite festive. Finally, in 1856, New England declared it a legal holiday.

The home and family—of utmost importance to the Victorians—were honored in every yuletide ritual. It was a time of wonder and magic for the children in particular. As Charles Dickens so aptly wrote, "My thoughts are drawn back, by a fascination which I do not care to resist, to my own childhood. I begin to consider, what do we all remember best upon the branches of the Christmas Tree of our own young Christmas days, by which we climbed to real life."

The Victorians took the greatest joy in romantic Christmas traditions and thoughtful details. In this hectic, modern-day world, it is no wonder that our most ideal images of Christmas are tied to nineteenth-century traditions. Restoring some of these beautiful customs will not only help keep our family heritage alive, but will greatly enhance the magic of the season as well.

"So guests were bidden, and musicians were engaged, and tables spread, and floors were prepared for active feet, and bountiful provision made of every hospitable kind. Because it was the Christmas season, and his eyes were all unused to English holly and its sturdy green, the dancing-room was garlanded and hung with it; and the red berries gleamed an English welcome to him, peeping from among the leaves."

CHARLES DICKENS

THE CHRISTMAS TREE

Charles Dickens relates the magic of the Christmas tree thus: "I have been looking on, this evening, at a merry company of children assembled round that pretty German toy, a Christmas Tree. The tree was planted in the middle of a great round table, and towered high above their heads. It was brilliantly lighted by a multitude of little tapers; and everywhere sparkled and glittered with bright objects."

The Christmas tree, that grandest holiday centerpiece, is largely recognized as a German tradition. In the sixteenth century, the Germans began observing the religious feast of Adam and Eve with a popular Christmas Eve play. Their main prop in the play was the Paradise tree—the tree of life—a fir tree decorated with apples, candles, cookies, and later, wafers.

In 1840, Queen Victoria began having a Christmas tree brought into the palace to make Prince Albert, her new German husband, feel at home. Eight years later, a famous engraving showed the queen with Albert and their children admiring the annual family tree, which had been decorated with candles, confections and paper chains. An angel topped the tree while toys and dolls awaited at the base. The custom of decorating a tree in the British home grew very fashionable from then on.

The Christmas tree took longer to catch on in America. It was still so rare by the mid-1800's that the main attraction at one bazaar was a "famous Christmas tree" which could be viewed for six-and-a-half cents. By the latter half of the century, however, the tree had become a fashionable American custom.

For most of the period, Victorian tree trimmings were homemade. The tree was often decorated with baked goods, strings of nuts, popcorn and cranberries, gingerbread figures, ribbons, candles (with a bucket of water nearby in case of fire), handcrafted paper flowers and garlands, gilded nuts, and cornucopias filled with candy. Pomander balls—oranges and lemons pressed with whole

cloves—were also hung from the branches. Shiny glass ornaments and tinsel did not become widely available until the late nineteenth century. It wasn't until the twentieth century that the Christmas tree candles were replaced by electric lights.

"O Christmas tree, O Christmas tree,
How lovely are your branches.
In summer sun, in winter snow,
A dress of green you always show.
O Christmas tree, O Christmas tree,
How lovely are your branches.

O Christmas tree, O Christmas tree,
With happiness we greet you.
When decked with candles once a year,
You fill our hearts with Yuletide cheer.
O Christmas tree, O Christmas tree,
With happiness we greet you."

TRADITIONAL GERMAN CAROL

Cookie Ornaments

Victorian cookie tree ornaments were somewhat thicker than today's cookies and were made from spice, butter or gingerbread recipes. They were often decorated with a sprinkling of red sugar. Traditionally they hung on the tree until it was taken down on Twelfth Night, and then they could finally be eaten.

To make cookie ornaments: Be sure the dough is well chilled before rolling it out. Cut into desired shapes with cookie cutters, and reroll the leftover dough for additional cookies. Make one hole at the top of each cookie with a plastic drinking straw. If the hole closes up after baking, use a toothpick to reopen it while still hot. Cool completely before decorating. If sprinkling sugar or applying decorations on top, brush the surface with slightly beaten egg whites or icing first. Tie a piece of ribbon in the hole of each cookie for hanging.

Handmade Victorian Ornaments

Victorian tree ornaments were usually handmade rather than store-bought. They could be baked, cut from paper, handcrafted out of wood, or sewn from fabric scraps. Favorite Victorian materials ranged from simple calicos to rich velvets, satins, and brocades. They were often stuffed and trimmed with lace, ribbons, crazy-quilt embroidery (a variety of embroidery styles mixed together), or beadwork.

Today, handmade ornaments are a gift in themselves and a treasured heirloom for the loved ones who receive

them. They can be stuffed into a stocking, or presented as a holiday favor at each table setting (a popular Victorian custom), or tucked atop Christmas gifts as decorative touches.

To sew your own ornaments: Cut some old-fashioned-looking fabric scraps into your favorite shapes, allowing extra material for a one-quarter-inch seam allowance. If desired, use a cookie cutter as your outline, and stick to simple shapes such as hearts, squares and circles. Apply desired needlework or beadwork to the surface before sewing the sides together.

With right sides facing each other, pin the decorated fabric together, including a ribbon loop for hanging at the top. If lace edging or border is desired, sandwich it between the two layers of fabric, making sure to turn edging

inward. Machine-stitch around the border of the ornament, leaving an inch or more open to turn material inside
out. Then stuff it and hand-stitch the opening closed.

Handsewn ornaments—especially non-seasonal shapes—
can be used year-round as pretty sachets, pincushions, or
brooch displays, depending on what they are filled with.
Stuff them with your favorite Victorian potpourri mixture—
perhaps dried roses, or lavender and rosemary mixed with
crushed cinnamon sticks—and they become sachets. Fill
them with bran—an old-fashioned stuffing—and they can
be used as decorative pin cushions. Or, omit the stuffing
altogether and place the ornament flat on your dresser to
display your favorite brooches.

WREATHS AND GARLANDS

Since ancient times, ever-
greens were thought to have mystical powers because they
remained green during the winter when other trees did
not. The practice of hanging greens in the house for good
luck during Christmas stems from this pagan belief—that
the world would regenerate for yet another year.

The Victorians welcomed Christmas as an opportunity
to dress up their homes in the spirit of the holidays. In
England and France, hanging holly over the doors symbol-
ized that the spirits were alive within. Generous green

garlands were draped everywhere—on the mantels, chandeliers, staircases, over the doorways, windows, and tall mirrors.

Looping swags of pine, bay, ivy and hemlock ropes was popular in Victorian homes. Rosemary—closely connected with the church and a token of remembrance—was also used. The pine-scented sprigs were often given as New Year's gifts to commemorate lasting ties. Juniper—the religious tree of refuge—was also honored at Christmastime.

The Christmas tradition of mistletoe evolved from a medley of old myths and eventually led to the English custom of kissing under it. For each kiss given, a berry was to be removed and presented to the lady kissed. When no berries were left the bough would lose its spell, and the maiden who received no kisses would not marry that year.

With a few basics, you can create Victorian wreaths and garlands to decorate your home or give as gifts. Use ivy or branches from your own evergreen shrubs—juniper, spruce, cedar, pine, and herbs such as bay, rosemary and lemon leaves.

Make sure your greens are fresh when you bring them into your home. Misting will help prevent them from drying out. Store them in a plastic bag in a cool place until ready to assemble. Buy a wire or straw wreath ring (available in hobby and florist shops), pruning clippers, and wire cutters. Also have paddle wire (gauge No. 28) on hand.

To make a wreath: Cut your evergreen boughs to

identical lengths, about 7 inches long. Place a handful of greens on the ring and use wire to tightly wrap them to the ring. Attach additional handfuls, using each to cover the ends of the previous attachment. When you have completed the circle, lift the top of the first handful and stuff the cut ends of the last handful underneath before wrapping. Add a large bow to conceal the connection. Use more wire to attach pine cones, bows, holly, or other ornaments.

You can accent evergreen wreaths with gilded objects of nature such as pine cones, nuts, seeds and pods, bay leaves, spices and dried fruits. Or, you can make a wreath entirely with gilded objects. Either dip the objects or spray them with metallic gold paint. Attach the objects to the wreath using hot glue.

With the above techniques, you can assemble garlands too. But instead of using a wire or straw ring, tie the evergreens to a length of dark-colored baler twine or nylon twine. Fasten one end of the twine to something secure so you can pull the cord taut as you work.

"The crisp leaves of holly, mistletoe, and ivy reflected back the light, as if so many little mirrors had been scattered there..."

CHARLES DICKENS

CHRISTMAS CARDS

Christmas cards date from the Victorian era, following the establishment of the one-penny postal service in 1840. The first commercially printed card was designed in the 1840's when an artist was commissioned to design a Christmas card for the friends of a London businessman. By the mid-nineteenth century, handmade cards were widespread. At first they were similar to Valentine cards, featuring bouquets of spring flowers, birds, and animals. Eventually, angels became a favored theme. The usual greeting then was the same as today: "A Merry Christmas and a Happy New Year to You."

Commercial Christmas cards became enormously popular from the 1870's on. One of the most widely published greeting card artists in the United States was Louis Prang, a German immigrant who was printing five million cards a year by 1881. Postmen grew so burdened during the holidays that the English press declared Christmas cards "a great social evil." But the seasonal sentiment continued to flourish right into the twentieth century.

"Our hearts they hold all Christmas dear,
And earth seems sweet and heaven seems near."

MARJORIE L.C. PICKHALL

THE VICTORIAN JOY OF GIVING

The Victorians were the first to begin exchanging gifts on Christmas Day. Before that it was traditional to give presents on New Year's or Twelfth Night. Boxing Day, or St. Stephen's Day, took place on December 26, when it was customary for working people such as house servants and tradesmen to open their gift boxes.

Gifts, both handmade and store-bought, were mostly given by parents to their children. The children would arise on Christmas morning to find little unwrapped presents tucked into their stockings. A sweet orange—considered an exotic treat in Victorian England—often filled the toe. Toy boats, soldiers, storybooks, and delicate, lifelike dolls might be found under the tree.

Simple gifts were sometimes exchanged between family members, lovers, and close friends. Popular nineteenth-century gifts included framed photographs, leatherbound books, lacy handkerchiefs, a brooch, watch, gloves, or lavender water—a favorite Victorian scent. Hand-embroidered linens, patchwork quilts, and knitted scarves or mittens were also cherished presents. The custom of contributing to charity at Christmas—a true gift from the heart—also developed in the Victorian era.

No matter how simple they are, a potpourri of small handmade gifts for your loved ones will evoke the Christmas spirit in the most heartfelt way possible.

Heirloom Picture Mats

For the Victorians, Christmas was a special time for the celebration of family and friendship. They took great pride in displaying their family photographs and treasured memorabilia in lovingly crafted frames.

You can create a whole gallery of heirloom pictures by covering the mats with fabric and decorative trim. Find some old-fashioned-looking fabric scraps and delicate lace to display your favorite photographs. Use an antique frame to enhance the look.

To make your own heirloom picture mat: Buy or cut your own mat from lightweight (preferably acid-free) cardboard. Make sure the opening—whether square, rectangular or oval— is the correct size for your chosen photograph.

Using a light amount of craft glue, center and adhere the fabric to one side of the mat. Carefully cut out the center, leaving $1/2$-inch allowance of extra material. Clip the center curves and corners. Fold the raw edges through the center and glue in place. Glue or tape the outer edges over the mat also.

Decorate the mat as desired with lightweight trim such as flat strips of lace, ribbons or bows. A lace doily with the center removed looks especially romantic and is best shown off against a contrasting color of fabric.

You can finish off the inside of the mat by covering it with a slightly smaller mat, using acid-free paper. Assemble the picture frame and glass to finish.

Victorian Patchwork Stockings

According to British legend, the custom of hanging Christmas stockings began in 300 A.D. when Saint Nicholas dropped some gold coins along with his gifts down a chimney. The coins would have fallen through the grate but were caught by a stocking that had been hung to dry on the hearth. Ever since then, children have been leaving their shoes or stockings to be filled on Christmas Eve.

A Christmas stocking made of random patchwork provides a novel variation to the Victorian crazy quilts (fabrics of assorted sizes appliquéd together and embroidered along the borders) that were so popular during the nineteenth century.

To make your own patchwork stocking: Leaving an extra ¼-inch seam allowance, cut desired stocking shape from one piece of muslin material. Cut an identical pattern for the backing, plus two pieces of matching fabric for the lining.

Select four or five old-fashioned fabrics such as moiré, velvet, paisley or calico cotton; cut them into narrow strips of assorted widths. Machine-stitch the first strip across the top of the muslin. (The edges of the strip should extend slightly beyond the muslin.) With right sides facing, position and sew the second strip at a somewhat cockeyed angle to the first strip. Smooth down the second strip and press. Continue adding each strip in the same manner, pressing each strip down after sewing and working your way down to the toe.

When the surface of the muslin is completely covered with patchwork, trim the edges evenly with the muslin. Embroider the borders, using a variety of stitches, if desired. Then, with right sides facing, sew the front and backing together, leaving the top open. Clip curves and turn the stocking right side out; press.

Sew a wide border of lace around the top of the stocking. Add a loop for hanging if desired.

Sew the two lining pieces together. With raw edges out, insert the lining into the stocking. Turn under raw edges along the top and slip-stitch them together; press again.

Lavender Water

Mix together 2 cups (16 fl. oz.) distilled water, ½ cup (4 fl. oz.) vodka, and 12 drops of pure essential oil of lavender.

Lavender water is a soothing addition to your bath, as it calms the nerves. When chilled, it is delightfully refreshing dabbed on your face and neck.

"There was a great deal of laughing and kissing and explaining, in the simple, loving fashion which makes these home-festivals so pleasant at the time, so sweet to remember long afterward..."

LOUISA MAY ALCOTT

"A Merry Christmas"

Christmas Potpourri

2 cups (16 fl. oz.) cedar chips or wood shavings
1 cup (8 fl. oz.) bay leaves
¼ cup (2 fl. oz.) dried rosemary leaves
10 whole cinnamon sticks, crushed slightly
10 whole nutmegs
2 tbsp. (1½ Br. tbsp.) each whole cloves, allspice and
   star anise
assorted pine cones and pods
1 oz. powdered orris root
6 to 10 drops oil of cinnamon

*Combine all ingredients. Store in a covered
container in a cool place for 2 to 3 weeks, stirring
or shaking every other day.*

GIFTS FROM A VICTORIAN KITCHEN

The Victorians were well known for their love of sweets, and this affection was at its peak during the Christmas season. Holiday preserves such as marmalade, jams and jellies were canned months in advance. In the fall, a morning was set aside for the preparation of the plum pudding and fruitcakes. By early December, the baking of cookies, cakes and breads had begun in earnest. Tempting aromas continued to drift from the kitchen throughout the season.

Among the most popular nineteenth-century Christmas treats were preserves, shortbread, cake-like gingerbread,

mulled wine or cider, and that great Victorian passion—plum pudding.

Darkly rich and fragrant with spices, English plum pudding dates back to Druid yuletide celebrations. The Victorians used a base of suet, bread crumbs and raisins. The pudding was usually laced with brandy or whiskey and stored for weeks in a cool cellar. On Stir-Up Sunday at the beginning of Advent, each family member took turns stirring the mixture for good luck. It was also customary to hide a small silver coin in the pudding as a surprise gift. On Christmas Day it was steamed or boiled in a mold, bag or basin, then flamed before serving.

Another Victorian Christmas tradition was shortbread, a thick, crisp butter cookie. In Scotland it was customary to offer shortbread to visiting friends during Hogmanay—the Scottish New Year. The heavy dough was baked in a round pan and cut into pie-shaped wedges. For a novel variation on traditional shortbread, try chilling the dough first; then roll it out, and cut out thick Christmas cookies.

All the tastes of Christmas are found in mulled wine, also known as claret cup or *glögg*. Made with oranges, cloves, cinnamon, sugar, brandy and claret (the English term for dry red wine), this mulled drink was a favorite Victorian Christmas punch. A non-alcoholic version can be made with cider.

Festively bundled and beribboned, edible gifts will say an old-fashioned Christmas to all your friends and family. You can even carry it one step further and assemble the gifts in pretty baskets with recipe cards, cookie cutters, spices, and other accessories.

Old-Fashioned Gingerbread

¼ lb. butter
1 cup (8 fl. oz.) boiling water
¾ cup (6 fl. oz.) sugar
1 cup (8 fl. oz.) molasses
3 eggs
2 cups (16 fl. oz.) flour
1½ tsp. (1 Br. tsp.) baking soda
½ tsp. salt
1 tsp. (¾ Br. tsp.) ground ginger
1 tsp. (¾ Br. tsp.) ground cinnamon
¼ tsp. ground allspice

Preheat oven to 350°F. Grease 3 to 4 miniature loaf pans. Place butter in a medium bowl. Pour boiling water over the butter to melt. Add sugar and molasses, mixing well. Add eggs.

In a separate bowl, combine the remaining ingredients, mixing well. Add to the liquid mixture and beat until smooth. Pour into prepared loaf pans. Bake 30 to 35 minutes.

"Had I but a penny in the world, thou shouldst have it for gingerbread."

WILLIAM SHAKESPEARE

Victorian Persimmon Pudding

3 persimmons (stems removed), puréed
2 tsp. (1½ Br. tsp.) baking soda
¼ lb. butter, softened
¾ cup (6 fl. oz.) sugar
2 eggs
2 tsp. (1½ Br. tsp.) lemon juice
¼ cup (2 fl. oz.) brandy
1 cup (8 fl. oz.) all-purpose flour
1 tsp. (¾ Br. tsp.) cinnamon
1 cup (8 fl. oz.) slivered almonds
1 cup (8 fl. oz.) raisins
whipped cream

Grease a 2-quart pudding mold. (A 2-lb. coffee can with a plastic lid works well, too.) Fill a large pan with enough water to come halfway up the sides of the mold. Bring water to a boil while preparing pudding.

In a small bowl, combine the persimmon purée and baking soda. Set aside until mixture becomes stiff.

In a large mixing bowl, cream the butter and sugar. Beat in eggs, lemon juice and brandy. Add persimmon mixture, flour and cinnamon. Then stir in the almonds and raisins.

Spoon the batter into the greased mold, leaving ⅓ of the top free for the pudding to expand. Cover with a snug lid or foil. Place mold in the pan of boiling water, preferably on a rack to allow water circulation under

the mold. Cover the pan and steam in gently boiling water for 2 hours. Remove from pan and let cool for a few minutes. Remove the pudding from its mold and cool slightly on a rack. Serve warm with a bowl of whipped cream on the side. For a flaming holiday presentation, heat 2 to 4 tbsp. brandy, pour around the base of the pudding, and light with a match. Serves 8.

   Note: This pudding can be made ahead, wrapped in foil, and given as a scrumptiously rich gift, accompanied by the above serving suggestions.

Dickens' Mulled Wine

1 bottle dry red wine
1 cup (8 fl. oz.) water
¼ cup (2 fl. oz.) brandy
3 tbsp. (2¼ Br. tbsp.) sugar

½ cup (4 fl. oz.) raisins
4 cinnamon sticks
¼ tsp. ground allspice
12 whole cloves

In a medium saucepan on low heat, simmer all ingredients together for about 30 minutes. Strain and pour into gift bottles, if desired, decorating the bottles with pretty labels and tying cinnamon sticks to the neck. Makes 3 half-bottles (375 ml.). Serve hot or cold with a slice of orange in each glass.

   Note: Since the flavor intensifies with shelf life, mulled wine is best consumed as soon as possible.

Almond Shortbread Cookies

½ lb. softened butter
1 tsp. (¾ Br. tsp.) vanilla
¼ tsp. almond extract
2 cups (16 fl. oz.) flour
½ cup (4 fl. oz.) powdered (icing) sugar
¼ cup (2 fl. oz.) granulated sugar
1 cup (8 fl. oz.) finely ground almonds

Cream butter, vanilla, and almond extract together in a medium mixing bowl. Sift flour, both sugars, and ground almonds into butter mixture and thoroughly blend. Wrap dough in plastic wrap and chill for at least 1 hour.

Preheat oven to 325°F. Roll chilled dough onto a lightly floured surface until it is about ¼ inch in thickness. Cut out desired Christmas shapes with cookie cutters. Reroll the leftover dough and cut more shapes. Place cookies on an ungreased cookie pan. Bake for 20 minutes, until shortbread is lightly golden. Makes 3 to 4 dozen cookies.

"Christmas won't be Christmas without any presents..."
LOUISA MAY ALCOTT
Little Women

Preserves

A well-stocked larder was considered of utmost importance in a Victorian household. One of the main staples, aside from pickled foods, was preserves—marmalades, jams and jellies. The summer fields yielded great crops of fruits and berries which later provided comforting winter confections to spread on hot buttered toast, muffins, scones, and crumpets. These jars of homemade preserves will still make delectable holiday gifts. The term marmalade originally applied to any confection made by boiling fruits with sugar to produce a thick mixture. The use of citrus fruits—particularly Seville oranges—came along in late eighteenth-century Scotland.

The concept of crushing or jamming the fruit with sugar resulted in the word "jam," and eventually expanded to include all confections except marmalades, creamy curds and smooth jellies.

Kumquat Marmalade

2 lbs. kumquats
2 cups (16 fl. oz.) water
4 cups (32 fl. oz.) sugar
2 tbsp. (1½ Br. tbsp.) orange liqueur

Wash kumquats and slice thinly, removing seeds and ends. Place in a stainless steel or copper pan. Add water. Bring to a boil. Cover. Reduce heat and gently

boil 15 to 20 minutes until peel is tender. Add sugar and mix well. Cook uncovered over medium heat, stirring constantly until thick, about 25 to 30 minutes. Turn off heat. Stir in liqueur. Follow canning directions in following recipe. Fills about four 6-ounce jars.

Cranberry-Blueberry-Apple Jam

½ lb. cranberries (fresh or frozen)
1 lb. blueberries (fresh or frozen)
½ lb. tart green apples, peeled, cored and diced
3 cups (24 fl. oz.) sugar
1 tsp. (¾ Br. tsp.) ground cinnamon
juice of 1 lemon
3 tbsp. (2¼ Br. tbsp.) rum

In a medium stockpot, simmer the berries, apples, sugar, cinnamon, and lemon juice together, stirring frequently for 35 to 45 minutes, until quite tender. Boil rapidly the last few minutes. Turn off heat and stir in the rum. Let cool, then pour jam into warm, sterilized ½-pint canning jars, leaving about ⅛-inch headspace. Remove air bubbles by running a rubber spatula around the inside of each jar once. Cover with sterilized lids and firmly screw on bands. Fills about four ½-pint jars.

Store in a cool, dry place and refrigerate after opening. Without pectin, these jams do not have a long shelf life and should be used within a few months.

A VICTORIAN CHRISTMAS FEAST

Even in the humblest Victorian homes there was no more bountiful meal than the one held on Christmas Day. The yuletide feast was originally meant to symbolically sustain families through the rest of winter, and the Victorians took its significance most literally.

In fine Victorian households the table was dressed up with glittering seasonal settings. Luxurious table linens included a white damask or lace tablecloth with trims of lace and ribbons. The silver centerpiece, or épergné, was filled with tiers of fruit and nuts. Boughs of greenery or ivy trailed among the many candles. At each place setting was a handwritten card with the guest's name in addition to a little holiday gift—a favorite Victorian custom. Large starched napkins were tied with ribbons or napkin rings. Silverware was polished, and the cut glasses shined.

The sideboard was covered with a vast array of dishes, most of which we would recognize at Christmas today: roast potatoes, spiced red cabbage, cranberries, home-made preserves, and carrots, peas or squash. Home-baked braided breads—symbolic of good fellowship—were also emphasized.

Although roast beef and Yorkshire pudding was the national dish of England, the parading of the turkey or goose was a favorite Christmas table tradition. Filled with

sage and onion, or oyster stuffing (oysters were inexpensive and plentiful then), the bird was often accompanied by a port, plum, or Madeira sauce.

At Victorian Christmas parties, guests were traditionally greeted with a glass of holiday cheer such as punch cup, mulled wine, or eggnog. Since hors d'oeuvres were not very fashionable in those days, dinner began promptly when all the guests had assembled.

A typical Victorian meal was a long affair, consisting of many courses. It usually started with a soup course, accompanied by a glass of sherry. Almonds—a recurring Christmas theme—were often featured in Victorian soups. Nineteenth-century cookbooks offered a wide selection of soup recipes.

It was the sumptuous desserts—some of them months in the making—that crowned a Victorian Christmas feast. Among the most popular desserts were mincemeat pie (a Christmas favorite for five hundred years), pumpkin pie, Eccles cake, Dundee cake (a baked version of plum pudding topped with cherries and almonds), soft gingerbread, dark fruitcake, countless varieties of holiday cookies, and shortbread. Twelfth Day cake, served on Twelfth Day, brought Christmas to a close. A pea or bean was hidden inside the cake to designate the king or queen for the day.

But no Victorian feast was considered complete without a pudding of some kind. Appearing in many forms, they ranged from Christmas plum pudding to custard to syllabub. Trifle, a layered confection, was described by Oliver Wendell Holmes as "that most wonderful object of domestic art...with its charming confusion of cream and

cake and almonds and jam and jelly and wine and cinnamon and froth." Served in a glass bowl to show off its colorful layers, trifle makes a perfect holiday dessert.

"...In half a minute Mrs. Cratchit entered flushed, but smiling proudly—with the pudding, like a speckled cannon ball, so hard and firm, blazing in half of half a quartern of ignited brandy, and bedight with Christmas holly stuck into the top."

CHARLES DICKENS

MENU

Almond Soup
Roast Turkey
Oyster Stuffing
Madeira Sauce
Roasted Potatoes
Spiced Red Cabbage
Peas with Mint
Raspberry Trifle

39

Almond Soup

1¼ cups (10 fl. oz.) ground almonds
4 cups (32 fl. oz.) chicken stock
½ tsp. white pepper
1 bay leaf
3 tbsp. (2¼ Br. tbsp.) butter
2 tbsp. (1½ Br. tbsp.) cornstarch
3 cups (24 fl. oz.) half and half
   (half cream, half whole milk)
½ cup (4 fl. oz.) sherry
salt to taste
¼ cup (2 fl. oz.) slivered almonds
chopped parsley for garnish

In a medium saucepan, simmer the ground almonds, half the stock, pepper and bay leaf for 30 minutes. Remove the bay leaf and purée the soup in a blender or food processor.

In a separate saucepan, melt the butter. Add the cornstarch and cook for a minute; then gradually add half and half, stirring constantly. Add remaining stock, almond purée, sherry and salt. Simmer for another 10 minutes.

Sauté slivered almonds in butter until golden brown; sprinkle almonds and chopped parsley over the soup before serving. Serves 6 to 8.

Oyster Stuffing

2 tbsp. (1½ Br. tbsp.) butter
4 tbsp. (3 Br. tbsp.) onions, chopped
1 cup (8 fl. oz.) raw oysters, chopped
4 cups (32 fl. oz.) bread crumbs
½ cup (4 fl. oz.) parsley, chopped
½ cup (4 fl. oz.) celery, chopped
1 tsp. (¾ Br. tsp.) dried tarragon
¾ tsp. (½ Br. tsp.) salt
½ tsp. hot paprika
dash cayenne pepper
⅔ cup (5⅓ fl. oz.) chicken stock
4 tbsp. (3 Br. tbsp.) butter, melted

Sauté onions in 2 tbsp. butter in a small pan until soft. In a large mixing bowl, combine the oysters, sautéed onions, bread crumbs, parsley, celery, tarragon, salt, paprika, and cayenne pepper. Stir in chicken stock and 4 tbsp. melted butter. Dressing should have a moist texture; if not, add more stock or melted butter. Refrigerate stuffing until ready to dress the turkey. After stuffing the cavity, press any remaining stuffing into an ovenproof bowl and bake with the turkey. Cook the turkey immediately after stuffing.

Spiced Red Cabbage

4 tbsp. (3 Br. tbsp.) butter
1 large onion, chopped
2 lbs. red cabbage, shredded
4 medium green apples, peeled, cored and chopped
½ tsp. ground cinnamon
¼ tsp. ground cloves
¼ cup (2 fl. oz.) brown sugar
⅓ cup (2⅔ fl. oz.) red wine
salt to taste

Melt butter in a large skillet over medium-high heat. Add onions, cabbage and apples. Sauté until tender, stirring frequently. Stir in cinnamon, cloves, brown sugar, red wine, and salt; cook until liquid is reduced. Serve hot or cold. Serves 8.

"I now have my house full for Christmas holidays, which I trust you also keep up in the good old style. Wishing a merry Christmas and a happy New Year to you and yours."

Washington Irving

Raspberry Trifle

Custard

3 cups (24 fl. oz.) milk
4 tbsp. (3 Br. tbsp.) cornstarch
2 tbsp. (1½ Br. tbsp.) sugar
2 egg yolks
1 tsp. (¾ Br. tsp.) vanilla extract

In a heavy 2-quart saucepan over medium heat, mix ½ cup (4 fl. oz.) milk and the cornstarch. Add remaining milk and sugar, stirring constantly until it thickens and comes to a boil. Remove from heat.

In a small bowl, beat egg yolks and a small amount of the custard mixture with a fork. Return to saucepan. Bring to a boil again. Boil 1 minute, stirring constantly. Remove from heat and add vanilla.

Note: You may prepare the custard and cake in advance and refrigerate until ready to assemble the trifle.

Trifle

1 12-oz. pound cake mix, baked according to directions
4 tbsp. (3 Br. tbsp.) good quality raspberry jam
1 cup (8 fl. oz.) slivered blanched almonds
1 cup (8 fl. oz.) medium dry drinking sherry
¼ cup (2 fl. oz.) brandy
2 cups (16 fl. oz.) heavy cream
2 tbsp. (1½ Br. tbsp.) sugar
2 cups (16 fl. oz.) fresh raspberries

Cut two or three 1-inch-thick slices of the cake and coat them with jam. Place slices in the bottom of a large glass bowl, jam side up. Cut remaining cake into 1-inch cubes and scatter them over the slices. On top of the cake sprinkle a half-cup of the almonds, then the sherry and brandy; let stand for 30 minutes.

Whip the cream, add sugar, then whip again until stiff. Set aside a few of the best-looking berries and pour the rest over the cake. Spread custard over the berries with a spatula. Add whipped cream last, and top with remaining berries and almonds.

"Christmas is here, Merry old Christmas,
Gift-bearing, heart-touching,
Joy-bringing Christmas, Day of grand memories,
King of the Year!"

WASHINGTON IRVING

GRAPHIC DESIGN BY GRETCHEN GOLDIE

PHOTO STYLING BY SUE TALLON

ACKNOWLEDGMENTS

PAMELA BARRUS, ELEANOR CHRISTENSEN, SYLVIA FOX,
LENA GLASS, BILL AND BECKY HABBLETT, LINDA LAMPSON,
ALMA MEIERDING, JOE POSHEK, SANDY ROSS, REBECCA SEGAL,
ROBIN AND BILL SMITH, ALVY TAYLOR TRYGG,
CHARLES AND JULIETTE TRYGG, AND ANNETTE WIRTZ